Hydroelectric Power

Power from Moving Water

Marguerite Rodger

Crabtree Publishing Company
www.crabtreebooks.com

Crabtree Publishing Company
www.crabtreebooks.com

Author: Marguerite Rodger
Editor: Lynn Peppas
Proofreader: Crystal Sikkens
Editorial director: Kathy Middleton
Production coordinator: Amy Salter
Prepress technician: Amy Salter
Produced by: Plan B Book Packagers
Developed and Produced by: Plan B Book Packagers

Photographs:
Shutterstock: Tyler Olson: cover; Serg64: title page; TebNad: p. 4;
Hywit Dimyadi: p. 5 (top); Glenda M. Powers: p. 5 (middle);
Darren Brode: p. 6 (bottom); Michael C. Gray: p. 6 (top); Chris
Kruger: p. 7 (bottom right); Thomas Moens: p. 7 (bottom left);
Zhuda: p. 7 (top); Tomasz Parys: p. 8; Nancy Hixson: p. 9 (top);
Cynthia Kidwell: p. 9 (bottom); Chester Tugwell: p. 10; V. J.
Matthew: p. 11 (bottom); N. Minton: p. 11 (top); Oleg V. Ivanov:
p. 12; Baloncici: p. 13 (top); James Steidl: p. 13 (bottom);
Tawfik Dajani: p. 14 (top); André Klaassen: p. 14 (bottom); Judy
Kennamer: p. 15; akva: p. 16 (top); Jose Gil: p. 16 (bottom left);
Timofeyev Alexander: p. 16 (bottom middle); Danny E Hooks:
p. 16 (bottom right); Patrick McCall: p. 17; Carmen Sorvillo:
p. 18 (top); Andriano: p. 18–19; Sascha Burkard: p. 20 (bottom);
William Casey: p. 20 (top); Jiri Slama: p. 21; Good Mood Photo:
p. 22; Terry Davis: p. 23; Thomas Barrat: p. 24 (top); Maridav:
p. 24 (bottom); Claudio Zaccherini: p. 25; Bond 80: p. 26 (bottom);
Losevsky Pavel: p. 26 (top); Vladyslav Danilin: p. 27 (bottom);
Lin, Chun-Tso: p. 27 (top); Lucian Coman: p. 28; Dancing
Rabbit Ecovillage: p. 29; K. Kulikov: p. 30 (top); Jason Yoder:
p. 30 (bottom); Justin Maresch: p. 31

Cover: A hydroelectric power plant on a fast moving river. Hydro plants often dam lakes to create reservoirs for making electricity.

Title page: Water rushes at a hydroelectric power dam.

Library and Archives Canada Cataloguing in Publication

Rodger, Marguerite
   Hydroelectric power : power from moving water /
Marguerite Rodger.

(Energy revolution)
Includes index.
ISBN 978-0-7787-2920-4 (bound).--ISBN 978-0-7787-2934-1 (pbk.)

1. Water-power--Juvenile literature. I. Title. II. Series:
Energy revolution

TC147.R63 2010   j333.91'4   C2009-906923-7

Library of Congress Cataloging-in-Publication Data

Rodger, Marguerite.
   Hydroelectric power power from moving water / Marguerite Rodger.
      p. cm. -- (Energy revolution)
   Includes index.
   ISBN 978-0-7787-2920-4 (reinforced lib. bdg. : alk. paper)
   -- ISBN 978-0-7787-2934-1 (pbk. : alk. paper)
   1. Water-power--Juvenile literature. I. Title.

TC147.R58 2010
621.31'2134--dc22
                                        2009048027

Crabtree Publishing Company

www.crabtreebooks.com   1-800-387-7650

Printed in the U.S.A./122009/CG20091120

Published in Canada
Crabtree Publishing
616 Welland Ave.
St. Catharines, ON
L2M 5V6

Published in the United States
Crabtree Publishing
PMB 59051
350 Fifth Avenue, 59th Floor
New York, New York 10118

Published in the United Kingdom
Crabtree Publishing
Maritime House
Basin Road North, Hove
BN41 1WR

Published in Australia
Crabtree Publishing
386 Mt. Alexander Rd.
Ascot Vale (Melbourne)
VIC 3032

Contents

Energy Conservation: "We Can Do It!"

"We Can Do It" was a slogan that appeared on posters made during World War II. One poster featured "Rosie the Riveter," a woman dressed in blue coveralls (shown below). The poster was originally intended to encourage women to enter the workforce in industry to replace the men who left to serve in the war. Today, the image of Rosie the Riveter represents a time when people came together as a society to reach a common goal. Today's energy challenge can be combatted in a similar way. Together, we can work to save our planet from the pollution caused by burning **fossil fuels** by learning to conserve energy and developing alternative energy sources.

What is Energy?

Energy is power. It is the force that gives us the ability to light our homes and schools. It powers our vehicles, and runs the equipment in our hospitals and factories. When we convert, or change energy into electricity, we can then use that electricity however we want. We use electricity every day. Try keeping track of how often you use electricity from the time you wake up in the morning to the time you get to school. You may be surprised at how much of an impact electricity has on your life!

Harnessing Energy

In order to use electricity, we must convert a natural source of energy into electricity. This can be done in many ways. Some natural sources of energy are burned, and the energy from the heat is converted, or changed, into electricity. Other natural resources, such as wind and water, do not necessarily need to be heated, but can be converted into electricity by using machines called **turbines** and **generators**.

Electic power lines transfer electricity to homes, schools, and businesses.

(below) Fossil fuels such as coal, are finite, or limited resources. There is only so much of them on the planet and one day we will run out of these fuel sources.

Renewable and Nonrenewable

There are several natural sources of energy. Some of these sources are renewable, and some are nonrenewable. A renewable source can be used again and again because it is always "renewed." Wind, water, the Sun are renewable sources of energy. These sources are not **depleted**, and will continue to exist after use. There are also several natural sources of energy that are not renewable. These sources are known as fossil fuels because they are natural resource fuels that were formed from the fossil remains of ancient plants and animals that have been buried underground for millions of years. Fossil fuels are finite, or limited, sources. This means that one day, they will run out. Coal, oil, and natural gas are fossil fuels.

We use electricity everyday to do things such as wash and dry laundry.

Conservation Tip

Try to wait until your clothes truly need to be washed before throwing them in the laundry hamper. Washing clothing after wearing only once is wasteful if the clothing is not dirty! When they are ready to be cleaned, use the cold water setting on your washing machine. It will reduce the amount of energy you use as there is no need to heat the water. It will also save your family money on the energy bill.

Our Energy Equation

Fossil fuels are the remains of prehistoric plants and animals that died 300 million years ago when Earth was warmer and covered in swamps and bogs! There is no way to recreate the conditions under which fossil fuels were made. Once we use up the supply, it will be gone forever.

Today, most countries use nonrenewable fossil fuel sources of energy to create electricity and to fuel vehicles and airplanes. Oil, natural gas, coal, and **peat**, will not last forever. We are using them up too quickly, and they are harming our environment.

Energy by Numbers

Fossil fuels took millions of years to make. At the rate that humans are currently using oil, supplies will run out in your lifetime. Scientists predict Earth's known supplies of oil will be depleted in about 50 years if we continue to use oil at the rate we do now. Imagine not being able to drive gas-powered cars in the future. Think about the world's entire fleet of airplanes being grounded because there is no fuel. Electricity outages will be common, as much of the world's electricity is powered by fossil fuels. The world as we know it will change and life will be a lot harder.

Petrochemical Lovers

We use fossil fuels such as oil and natural gas not only for power but also to manufacture thousands of different household products. The United States is home to one of the largest **petrochemical** industries in the world. This industry is responsible for transforming oil, natural gas, and coal into petrochemicals. Petrochemicals are used to make plastic, paint, rubber, synthetic materials, and even some drugs.

This playground equipment is made from petrochemical plastics.

Making the Switch

Conserving fossil fuel energy sources and switching to renewable energy sources are the only options for the future. Conserving will make the dwindling supplies last longer. Switching to renewable energy sources will ensure that we have other sources of power for the future. Renewable energy sources, also called alternative energy, do less harm to the environment.

Global Warming and Fossil Fuels

Global warming is the increase in the average temperature of Earth. Most scientists believe this temperature increase is caused by the excess gases released when using fossil fuels. When coal, oil, and gas are burned, they emit a number of chemicals and gases, including carbon dioxide (CO_2), methane, water vapor, nitrous oxide, and ozone. These gases are naturally present in Earth's atmosphere. They help absorb some of the Sun's harmful rays and keep Earth's temperature at a level that supports life. Burning fossil fuels increases the amount of these gases in the atmosphere, trapping them there and warming Earth. Climate conditions caused by global warming include the melting of polar ice caps and rising ocean levels. Global warming has also been blamed for droughts in some areas of the world.

Droughts caused by global warming lead to habitat destruction and mass starvation.

Carbon Culture

North Americans use more barrels of oil each year than people on any other continent. They also create more pollution per capita, or per person. North Americans leave a very large "carbon footprint" on Earth. A carbon footprint is a way of measuring the impact, or effect, of human activities on the environment and climate change. A footprint measures all the greenhouse gases individuals produce through their daily activities. For example, if you live in a very large house that is heated and cooled using fossil fuels, and you travel a lot in automobiles and planes, your carbon footprint will be larger than someone who conserves energy and takes the bus or walks.

Carbon Addicts

Both individuals and large businesses use energy from fossil fuels everyday. About 95 percent of the world's energy comes from fossil fuels. Over 65 percent of the world's electric power comes from fossil fuels. Coal is a cheap fuel. About 93 percent of the coal produced in the United States is burned to generate electricity. The other seven percent is used as a source of power in factories that produce steel, paper, and concrete.

Big Footprint

On average, each person in the world creates four tons (four tonnes) of carbon dioxide every year. In North America, each person creates nearly 20 tons (20 tonnes) of carbon dioxide every year. We do this mostly by using a lot of electricity, traveling in planes, and driving in cars. Burning fossil fuels for transportation contributes to more than 13 percent of all greenhouse gas emissions.

Coal is widely used to generate electricity in the United States. Here, it powers a steel manufacturer's blast furnace.

The Amish use horsepower to get them from place to place.

Life Without Electricity

The Old Order Amish are a Christian group that lives apart from the modern world. They do not drive motorized vehicles and their houses do not have electricity. The Amish are mostly farmers, whose communities in the United States and Canada are known for their strong family bonds. They believe their simple way of life brings them closer to God. The Old Order Amish use horse and buggies for transportation but some hire cars driven by non-Amish or take public buses to places too far to travel by horse. Some Old Order communities also allow their members to use electricity generated by windmills on their farms. The Amish way of life creates a small footprint, because they use very little fossil fuels. They live the way farm people did over 100 years ago, before electricity and automobiles became common. Life is less convenient for them, but many non-Amish are starting to see the benefit of not being dependent on fossil fuels.

A windmill outside an Amish barn.

Energy from Water

Water is an important and often overlooked source of energy. Water is **versatile**. The energy created by movement of water can be turned into electricity using many methods.

Hydroelectricity

Hydroelectricity is electricity that uses the energy from moving water. Hydro is a Greek word meaning water. Hydroelectricity is a renewable resource because the water is not used up in order to make electricity. In fact, the same water can be used over and over again.

Geothermal Energy

Geothermal power uses the heat from Earth's core and converts it into electrical power. Geo is a Greek word meaning earth, while therme means heat. Earth's center is very hot, and consists of a hot liquid called magma. In some areas of the world, holes are drilled into the earth and geothermal steam rises. This steam is harnessed to drive turbines and generators in power plants. Geothermal can also be used to heat buildings directly, or be pumped into buildings using geothermal heat pumps.

Tidal Energy

If you live by an ocean, you may notice how the water rises and lowers each day. This is called the tide. The energy generated by the water's tides is another way electricity is made from the power, or energy, of water. The Sun, the Moon, and Earth's gravity control the tide, which mean that tides are a very reliable resource. Tidal energy can be converted into electrical energy at tidal generating stations. Here, the energy is harnessed using power turbines, similar to the way wind can move the blades of a windmill. Dam-like **barrages** also channel the energy from flowing tides and convert it into electricity.

Geothermal heat can be carried to the surface of Earth at hot springs like this one.

Hydroelectric power can be harnessed from geothermal sources.

Harnessing Tidal Power

The Annapolis Royal Generating Station is located in Nova Scotia, Canada. It is the only tidal generating station in North America. The largest straight-flow turbine in the world is used at the Annapolis Royal Generating Station. The turbine uses the energy released from the rising tides of the Bay of Fundy to make electric power. Annapolis Royal is a town located near the Bay of Fundy, a bay known for having the largest vertical tidal range in the world. This means that the Bay of Fundy has enormous water level changes from high tide to low tide—rising an average of over 39 feet (12 meters) in 13 hours from low to high tide! Every year, the station is able to generate enough electricity to power 4,500 homes.

Twice a day, the Bay of Fundy is filled with 100 billion tons (tonnes) of seawater. When the tide goes out at low tide, fishing boats gradually lower to the bay floor like toys in a bathtub after the plug is pulled. The power of the tides is harnessed to generate electricity.

11

Hydroelectricity

Hydroelectricity is any electricity created using the energy contained in water. Water has energy because it is always moving—down the river with the current, with daily tides, or from flowing over a waterfall. This energy in motion is called kinetic energy.

Niagara Falls generates hydropower for New York State and Ontario by diverting water from the Niagara River. The United States and Canada have an agreement to restrict the amount of water diverted, or taken from Niagara Falls, so that the beauty is not lost in the quest for electric power.

Falling Water

Water's movement, or kinetic energy, has the potential to be turned into electricity. The faster water moves, or the higher the height from which it falls, the more electricity can be produced. One of the most productive waterfalls for electricity conversion is found at Niagara Falls, bordering the United States and Canada. These waterfalls, which are over 167 feet (51 meters) high, are the source of up to 6 million cubic feet (169,901 m³) of falling water every minute. The falls are harnessed for power by electric companies on both sides of the border.

Converting Energy

Water's energy is made into electricity using machines. Often when we talk about hydroelectricity, we think of dams, and the hydropower plants that are used to convert the water's energy into electricity. Using the power of a river's current is only one of many ways that hydroelectricity is made. Water can be turned into steam, which can power machines. Energy can also be found in the rise and fall of waves and tides.

Turbines convert the kinetic energy of water into energy for electricity.

Energy Star

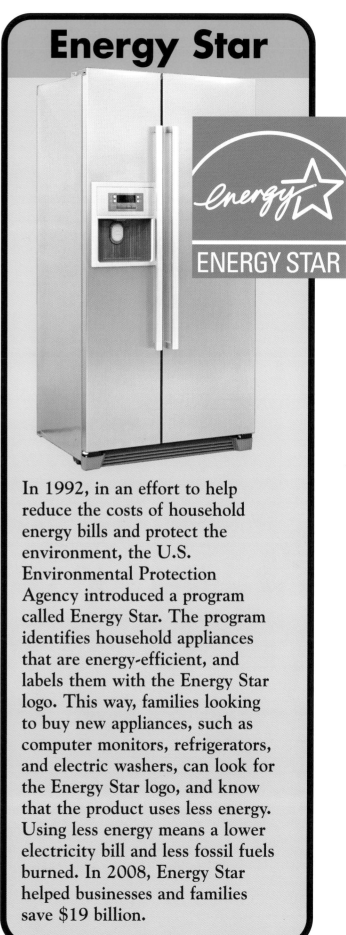

In 1992, in an effort to help reduce the costs of household energy bills and protect the environment, the U.S. Environmental Protection Agency introduced a program called Energy Star. The program identifies household appliances that are energy-efficient, and labels them with the Energy Star logo. This way, families looking to buy new appliances, such as computer monitors, refrigerators, and electric washers, can look for the Energy Star logo, and know that the product uses less energy. Using less energy means a lower electricity bill and less fossil fuels burned. In 2008, Energy Star helped businesses and families save $19 billion.

Hydro History

Water power has been used for thousands of years. In 700 BC, the noria, or Egyptian water wheel was used to **irrigate** crops. This large wooden wheel sat with its bottom half submerged in the Nile River. The river's current would cause the wheel to turn, dipping clay pots attached to it into the stream. When the pots reached the top of the wheel, they tipped over into a trough that would carry the water away to be used in nearby fields.

Ancient Mills

In Ancient Greece, over 2,000 years ago, water wheels similar to the noria were used to grind grain into flour. As the water wheel turned with the current, the wheel would turn gears. The gears then moved large stones that ground the grains into flour. These types of water wheels are called mills, and they are an important example of one of the ways that water power helped reduce the amount of work for people. People no longer had to grind grain by hand. Using the power of the water was much more efficient.

Ancient water power technology is still used to water farm crops in Egypt.

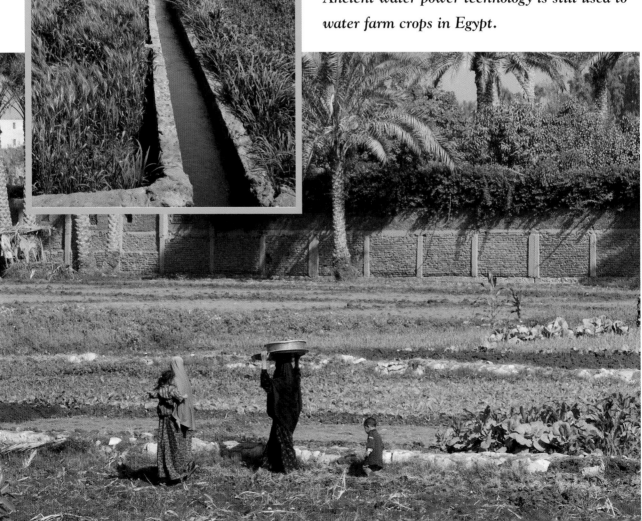

(above) The development of useful steam power in the 1770s allowed manufacturing industries to sprout up anywhere. Prior to this, water wheels were located on ponds, rivers, and lakes. Industries had to be located beside these prime sources of water power.

Water Does The Work

In the **Middle Ages**, the energy of moving water was used for many tasks including sawing wood, crushing vegetable seeds to make oils, and cleaning wool. It was even used to power simple machines, such as the bellows, a device that can blow air and was often used to fuel a fire.

Industrial Revolution

From the late 1700s to mid 1800s, the development of steam power led to what is now known as the **Industrial Revolution**. Before the Industrial Revolution, farms relied on manual labor, or the physical work of men and women, to harvest crops. Most goods were handmade in small workshops.

Steam Power

With the development of the steam engine and steam power, factories began to use machinery that converted coal and sometimes wood into fuel. Machines could do the work of many humans faster and more efficiently. Steam powered machines were used in the **textile** industry and cotton mills. Steam also powered farm machinery such as mechanical seeders, threshers, tractors, and harvesters. These machines meant farms needed fewer laborers. Many out-of-work laborers went to the cities to work in factories. This changed the way people lived as well as where, and how they lived. Steam power ushered in a new age of transportation as well, as steam trains replaced horse carriages and made is easier to travel great distances.

Mills of Industry

In the United States, the change from horse powered machinery to water powered machinery meant a leap in manfacturing production. In 1790, Samuel Slater, a man known as the founder of the American cotton industry, built the first American textile mill on the Blackstone River in Rhode Island. Not long after that, over 1,000 mills were powered by the powerful waters of the Blackstone River. It became known as "America's hardest working river." At this time, factories and towns were being built on land that was located near fast moving rivers, often on the Northeast coast of the country. Around 1860, after the **Civil War**, steam power became more popular than water power, allowing manufacturers to set up shop across the nation instead of just near fast moving rivers.

Bulb of Light

In the late 1800s, factories were powered by steam, but light for factories, city streets, and homes was still provided by candles, oil lanterns, and gas lights. Throughout that century, inventors struggled to produce an **incandescent** light bulb that would not burst after a few minutes of use. In 1879, Thomas Edison invented a long-lasting light bulb. The bulb was powered by electricity, and was able to last over 1,200 hours. In 1880, at the Wolverine Chair Factory in Grand Rapids, Michigan, 16 bulb lamps were lit using electricity generated from a water turbine. Two years later, in 1882, the first U.S. hydroelectric power plant was up and running on the Fox River in Wisconsin.

Before electric lighting was common, gas lamps were lit by hand every night in cities.

The incandescent light bulb was used for over 100 years before energy efficient compact fluorescent bulbs were created.

Thirst for Water Power

The next important step in the development of hydropower was to build large and powerful dams. Dams block rivers and use the **gravitational** force of water to generate electricity. In the 1930s, the U.S. began to build many large dams. Hoover Dam, located on the border between Arizona and Nevada, was built in just less than five years, and was completed in 1936. It spans an astonishing 726 feet (221 meters) in height and 1244 feet (379 meters) in length! It is made of concrete, and when it was built, was the largest concrete structure in the world. At that time, the Hoover Dam was also the largest electric-power generating station!

Power Plants

Today, the demand for electricity is too large to be powered solely by dams, but dams remain important because of their efficiency. Hydroelectric plants that use dams can convert 90 percent of water's energy into electricity, while nonrenewable sources such as coal-burning power plants may only convert up to 50 percent of their energy into electricity!

(above) Hoover Dam was an engineering marvel of the 1930s. Dams use reservoir water to turn turbine blades and generate power.

Conservation Tip

All over North America, homes and offices are making the switch from single incandescent light bulbs to compact fluorescent bulbs (CFLs). Incandescent bulbs create a lot of heat. Compact fluorescent bulbs use one quarter of the energy and last at least five years.

Generating Power

Hydroelectric power creates about ten percent of the world's electricity. Unlike fossil fuel powered electricity, which accounts for most of the electricity consumption in the United States, hydroelectric power does not contribute to global warming. How is water energy converted into hydroelectric power that we can use? How does it go from flowing water to powering a light bulb?

(right) Hoover Dam's concrete and steel intake towers sit in Lake Mead, right next to the dam. Intake towers control the water supply that turns the power plant turbines.

(below) A hydroelectric dam reservoir and concrete dam.

Energy Drain!

Many hydropower plants use dams to create large **reservoirs** of water that can be used at any time to create electricity. A dam is a barrier that stops or blocks the flow of water in a river or body of water. There are several steps for turning the water's energy into electricity:

1. Water that has been stored in a reservoir travels through underground gates, called the "intake," into large pipes, called "penstocks."

2. As the water travels from the large reservoir through the penstock, it builds up pressure.

3. The penstocks lead the running water to turbines that have been built deep inside the dam. Turbines have large blades, similar to a fan. The water flows past the turbine, and the blades begin to turn. The turbine is attached to a large generator.

4. When the blades of the turbine turn, so do several magnets inside the generator. The generator is the machine in the hydropower plant that produces the electricity. The magnets inside the generator are very large, and as they rotate past a copper coil, they move many electrons around. This produces **alternating current** (AC).

5. The AC then flows into a transformer. Transformers are used to turn the AC into a higher-voltage current. Higher voltage costs less because it travels very efficiently.

6. The electric current then travels out of the hydropower plant through power lines.

7. The last and final step is outflow. Once the water has completed its journey through the hydropower plant, it is carried through pipelines called "tailraces," which take the water back into the river downstream.

How Much Power?

How much electricity can a hydropower plant make? The answer can vary, depending on the type of hydropower plant. There are three types of hydropower plants: high head, run-of-the-river, and pumped storage. The amount of water that flows through the power plant and the height from which it falls determine the amount of electricity that is made.

How High?

High head means that the water is falling from a height greater than 500 feet (152 meters). These types of hydropower plants create the most energy because huge amounts of water are falling into the power plant from a great height. Run-of-the-river means that the power plant did not create a reservoir, but instead allows the natural flow of the river to push the water through the intake gates. Pumped storage facilities have both an upper and a lower reservoir. Once the water leaves the power plant, it enters the lower reservoir, and is then pumped back to the upper reservoir through a reverse turbine to be used again!

Transformers and power lines move the electricity from where it is generated to where it is used, such as your home or school.

Conservation Tip

The more energy we waste, the more we need to generate. Have you ever thought about how much energy is wasted on a daily basis? Even from the very source—the power plants—energy is being wasted. When the energy leaves the power plants in the form of electricity, up to 75 percent of the fuel that was used to create the electricity has already been lost. We are wasting energy to make electricity. The less electricity we use, the less we waste!

Canada is a land of abundant rivers and abundant hydroelectric power. Many rivers are harnessed or dammed to provide power. Canadian hydropower is even sold to the United States.

Power by Numbers

In Canada, the most important source of electricity is moving water. In 2009, it accounted for almost 60 percent of the country's electricity supply. In fact, hydropower is so common that when most Canadians talk about electricity bills, they use the term "hydro bill." The second most important source of electricity in Canada is fossil fuels. Roughly 16.5 percent of electricity currently comes from coal, 5.2 percent from natural gas, and 1.9 percent from petroleum. Over 15 percent of the country's electricity comes from nuclear power, while the remaining electricity (less than two percent) comes from renewable resources other than water, such as wind and sunlight. In the United States, hydroelectric power supplied the country with just over six percent of total electricity. Over three percent of the country's power comes from other renewable sources. Fossil fuels contribute the majority of the electricity that is consumed in the United States. Coal supplies a whopping 49 percent of electricity to the country, while natural gas and nuclear energy account for roughly 20 percent each.

Pros and Cons of Dams

Hydroelectric power dams are concrete walls that cross rivers, blocking the natural flow of water. Dams create reservoirs that are necessary to power hydropower plants, but their construction comes at a price. Environmentalists say massive dam projects destroy **ecosystems** and animal habitats, cause flooding, and displace human communities.

Flooding

Dam reservoirs are artificial lakes created when a river is blocked. Reservoirs for large dam projects can flood many miles of land where humans and animals live. When completed in 1970, the Aswan High Dam on the Nile River in Egypt forced 60,000 people from their homes and flooded ancient archaeological sites. On the positive side, the dam also prevented the river's yearly floods and provided power for half of Egypt, including villages that never had power.

Erosion

Dams also cause riverbank and shoreline erosion. Normally, as rivers flow downstream, he water carries sediment or silt. These small particles of soil are like underwater dust. The current carries the sediment to another part of the river, where it settles on the bottom of the riverbed. Dams stop the sediment and silt from traveling to new parts of the river. Instead, the silt and sediment remain in one location, and collect over time. This buildup can pose a threat to the fish and underwater vegetation. At the same time, the riverbed downstream is being deprived of the sediment, and erosion, or a breakdown of the soil, occurs.

Thousands of caribou drowned in northern Quebec in 1984 when a dam project altered their habitat.

Habitats Change

Dam building and reservoir flooding can be devastating to animal habitats. Reservoirs cause water temperature changes to rivers that flow into them. Even a slight temperature change can make it hard for some species of fish to spawn. Dams also disrupt the migration of fish such as salmon, who must swim upstream to lay their eggs. In 1984, over 10,000 caribou drowned in northern Quebec after heavy rains spilled over a dam at a James Bay hydroelectric project. The caribou were following their annual migration route across two rivers.

Fish ladders provide salmon with a set of underwater stairs. These allow them to jump upstream around a dam, to lay their eggs.

Action for Rivers

Every year on March 14, people from all over the world gather to speak out against the construction of dams. The International Day of Action for Rivers began in 1997 in Curitiba, Brazil, at the First International Meeting of People Affected by Dams. Several groups of people from all over the world meet each year to discuss and protest the negative impact that the construction of dams can have. They discuss issues such as pollution, the destruction of indigenous communities, and press governments to let local communities have a say in what happens to their rivers.

Three Gorges

The Three Gorges Dam project took many years to build and displaced people and animals.

The dam reservoir has made it easier for ships to navigate the Yangtze River.

Located on the Yangtze River in China, the Three Gorges Dam is the largest electricity-generating plant in the world. Planning for the dam began in 1932, but construction did not begin until the 1990s.

Costly Dam

Three Gorges Dam has an estimated cost of $30 billion. The cost to the environment and to human lives cannot be measured. The dam's reservoir is 373 miles (600 kilometers) long! The hydropower plant has 34 generators, with a capacity of 17 million kilowatts, that supply power to central China. China is growing rapidly, and is quickly becoming the largest consumer of coal in the world. Hydroelectricity may help reduce their fossil fuel use.

Controversial Project

One of the reasons that the Three Gorges Dam has taken so long to complete is that it is a very controversial project. Many people did not want the dam to be built. Over 262 square miles (679 square km) of land were flooded to create the reservoir. Over one million people living near the dam were forced to relocate. As with other dams, the ecosystem has also been effected. The area that was flooded was home to many different species, including the endangered Siberian Crane. After dam construction began in 1994, the already endangered Baiji, or Yangtze River dolphin, went from a known population of 300 to just 14. Many archaeological digs and historical landmarks have been lost to reservoir flooding.

Power to a Nation

The reservoir has also created a safer route for shipping. Many boats had difficulty navigating the once dangerous river, but the construction of the dam has included the installation of ship locks and lifts, or devices that raise boats around the dam. Now that boats are able to safely travel down the river, they are used more often to transport goods. This is far more energy efficient than trucks, and using boats instead of trucks reduces greenhouse gas emissions.

The Three Gorges dam supplies power to many of China's bustling cities.

Conservation Tip

Have you ever heard of "standby power"? This is a term used to describe the power that is being used by appliances when they are not in use, but are still running or plugged in. Try walking around your house and take note of all the little red lights you see on the stereo, the DVD player, and computer monitor. You may not be watching the television, or surfing the Internet, but your appliances might still be on, wasting power and fossil fuels. Take some time to turn off, unplug, and save some power!

Hydro's Future

Hydroelectric dams control the flow of water and harness the power of rivers. Most hydroelectic power is produced this way but there are other forms of hydroelectricity. These alternative sources of hydroelectricity are important because they are more efficient and less harmful to the environment.

Damless Hydro

A very important part of hydropower plants is the turbine. Turbines are used to convert the water's energy into electricity. The faster the water moves, the more electricity that can be made. Most often, dams are built to control the flow of rivers, forcing the water to move through the turbine. However, damless hydroelectricity is also a possibility. If a turbine is placed in a river where the current is naturally quick, the energy can be harnessed from the moving water without the construction of a dam. This prevents damage such as flooding, that is caused when dams are built on rivers.

Micro Hydro

Micro hydro refers to small hydroelectric power generators that can produce up to 100 kilowatts of power. Micro hydro can often be generated from small but fast flowing streams of water. For example, some small but powerful waterfalls can be used to create micro hydro. The pool of water at the top of the waterfall works as the reservoir, and several hundred feet of pipe can be used to help gather and direct the water to a small generator. This type of hydroelectricity is called run-of-the-river. It does not require a dam or reservoir. Micro hydro is most often used in developing countries to supply hydro to small communities. Smaller generators, called pico hydro, generate under five kilowatts of power. They are used in remote areas of the world to power light bulbs or batteries.

Pico hydro generators can provide enough power for electric lightbulbs or small appliances in remote villages all over the world.

Living Off the Grid

Living "off the grid" means living without power produced by major utility companies. The electrical grid is a system or network of interconnected transmission lines that brings electrical power from the supplier (power companies) to the users (consumers). People who live off the grid either do not use electric power at all, or they make their own micro-generated power from renewable sources such as windmills and solar panels. Dancing Rabbit Ecovillage in Missouri, is a community of people that decided to put the environment first and live low-impact lifestyles. Each home in the Dancing Rabbit Ecovillage is built from recycled or low-impact environmental materials. Homes are also equipped with renewable energy systems. Electricity is supplied by solar and wind power. The village takes care of its own water supply and waste disposal. Ecovillage residents also conserve energy and use energy efficient appliances. About 45 people live in Dancing Rabbit, but residents hope it will someday grow to over 1,000, with all the energy needs supplied by renewable sources. Dancing Rabbit is an intentional community, which means that the people who live there designed it with a common idea of sustainability and cooperation between neighbors. You do not have to live in an ecovillage to live off the grid. In North America, people who live off the grid make a commitment to using alternative energy sources for their power. Throughout the world, an estimated 1.7 billion people live without electricity, but most of them have no other choice.

Doing Your Part

Changing our energy use, or consumption habits is an easy way to help the environment. There are many things we can do to save energy and reduce our fossil fuel dependence. Our bad habits can be fixed with small changes in our daily routines. When you add up the positive effects of several energy saving habits, they will contribute to fixing a much larger problem!

Be a Good Consumer

Following the conservation tips throughout this book can help you make decisions that reduce your carbon footprint and have a good impact on our Earth. Here are some more simple ideas to help reduce the impact of our energy use:

1) Suggest that your parents use pot lids when cooking on their stovetop. This reduces the amount of energy that you need from the stove by trapping the heat in the pot.

2) Think about your use of small electronic appliances. Cell phones, video games, flat screen televisions, and other devices account for 15 percent of household power demand. This will only increase in the future. Encourage your parents to use smart power strips to power up these gadgets.

3) Dry your clothes on an indoor or outdoor clothesline. Hanging clothes is also a chore that you can do to help your parents out. Clothing driers use a lot of electricity. Clothes dried "on the line" smell fresh and clean too!

4) Write letters to appliance manufacturers, asking them to make products that use energy more efficiently. Most video game consoles, for instance, make it difficult to save games now, so they are not switched off to save power. Ask manufacturers to do their part!

5) Join an environmental organization for kids, or start one yourself. Melissa Poe of Nashville, Tennessee, started her own environmental group when she was nine years old! Her group, Kids For A Clean Environment (Kids FACE or www.kidsface.org) started with six members in 1989. It now has over 300,000 members and has distributed and planted over one million trees.

Trees help absorb CO2, so planting trees is good for the environment.

Use rechargeable batteries to save energy and waste.

28

Small changes can add up to big energy and environment savings. Solar panels use heat from the Sun. White roofs keep homes cool in the summer.

CASE STUDY

Energy Efficient School

Schools can save energy, too! In 2007, Mohawk College in Hamilton, Ontario, started an energy-efficient replacement program. The program replaces low-efficiency appliances and lights in the school with newer energy-saving equipment. The school began by switching more than 8,600 old fluorescent lights to energy efficient, high performance bulbs. This single change cut the province's energy demands by 99,000 kilowatt-hours, and saved the school $12,000 on its energy bills in the first 90 days. This is just the first step in the school's plan to save energy. Exit signs above doors have been replaced with Light Emitting Diode (LED) exit signs. These signs use 90 percent less energy than the older models. The plan also includes the replacement of the air conditioning units and the boilers. The program will cost $10 million, but will save more money and energy in the long term.

Timeline

Water has played an important part in the history of the world. In the ancient world, water's energy was used to operate simple machinery. Today, water is being used to save the planet, as the shift is made from fossil fuels to renewable energy sources.

Power lines are a common sight throughout North America.

Water has powered mills for centuries.

146 BC

Water mills are used in Ancient Greece to grind grain, reducing physical labor for humans.

1300s

In Europe, water power continued to be used to power mills, and was also used to power simple machines, such as the bellows.

1700s

The use of steam power in factories and on farmland contributes to what is now known as the Industrial Revolution in Great Britain.

1759

Daniel Joncaire built a small canal above Niagara Falls to power his sawmill. This is the first attempt made to use the power of this famous waterfall.

1878

The first household to be lit using hydroelectricity is the Cragside House in Northumberland, England.

1880

Electricity is used to power lights in the Wolverine Chair Factory, Michigan, USA.

1881

Street lamps in Niagara Falls, New York, are lit by hydropower.

1882

The first U.S. hydroelectric power plant opens in Fox River, Wisconsin.

1893

Alternating Current (AC) is used in hydropower plants in the U.S. for the first time.

1936

The construction of the Hoover Dam is complete.

1940s

World use of fossil fuels for energy and transportation grows.

1945

Hydroelectricity accounted for 94 percent of Canada's electricity generation. Today, it is roughly two-thirds of all electricity generation in Canada.

1950s

Climate scientists start noticing a rise in Earth's average temperature. This continues to rise over the next several decades.

1997

Kyoto Protocol adopted in Japan on December 11. It is an international treaty on climate change that calls for the reduction of greenhouse gases.

1991

Construction of the Itaipu Dam in Brazil is completed. It remains the largest hydroelectricity generating plant in South America, and second largest in the world, next to the Three Gorges Dam in China.

2009

About seven percent of all U.S. electricity comes from hydropower.

2011

Construction to be completed on the world's largest hydroelectric dam, the Three Gorges Dam on the Yangtze River in China.

Wind farms harness energy from wind to provide alternative electrical power.

Glossary

alternating current An electric current that reverses its direction or alternates several times a second

barrages Obstructions that stop the flow of water

Civil War A war (1861-1865) in the United States, between the Union states of the north, and the Confederate states of the south. It was fought over the issues of state rights and slavery

depleted Exhausted, or used up

drought A prolonged period of little or no rainfall resulting in a shortage of water

ecosystem A natural physical environment where plants and animals interact

fossil fuels Fuels found in Earth's crust that are non-renewable sources of energy

generator A machine that generates or makes power

gravitational The movement, or pull, of something toward a center of attraction. Also, the force of attraction given by each part of matter in the universe

incandescent Emitting light when heated. An electric light containing a filament that glows hot and produces light when heated by a current of electricity

indigenous Originating from, or native to, a particular place

Industrial Revolution A period of rapid change and industrial development that occurred in Britain in the late 1700s and other places a little later. Many new machines were invented during this time that allowed goods to be mass produced

irrigate To supply water to land for crops

Middle Ages A period of European history that runs roughly from 1100 AD to 1453 AD

peat A fuel produced of decomposed plant matter found in bogs. It is cut and dried and can be burned

petrochemicals Chemical materials such as paints, pesticides, and plastics made by refining and processing oil and natural gas

reservoir A large lake used as a supply of water for hydroelectric plants

textiles Cloth or woven fabrics

turbines A wheel or rotor machine used for producing power. It has blades that revolve very fast with flows of water, steam, or air

versatile Adaptable, or able to perform many functions

Index